STALKING THE STALKER

STALKING THE STALKER

Fighting Back with High-tech Gadgets and Low-tech Know-how

Diane Glass

iUniverse, Inc.

New York   Lincoln   Shanghai

Stalking the Stalker
Fighting Back with High-tech Gadgets and
Low-tech Know-how

Copyright © 2006 by Diane Glass

iUniverse books may be ordered through booksellers or by contacting:

iUniverse
2021 Pine Lake Road, Suite 100
Lincoln, NE 68512
www.iuniverse.com
1-800-Authors (1-800-288-4677)

WRpress

Cover art by Don Synstelien Designs
Cover design by Dan Wooten Designs
Author photo by Linda Rathke Photography

ISBN-13: 978-0-595-38332-0 (pbk)
ISBN-13: 978-0-595-82704-6 (ebk)
ISBN-10: 0-595-38332-7 (pbk)
ISBN-10: 0-595-82704-7 (ebk)

Printed in the United States of America

To Leif

Contents

Chapter One

Introduction

I hate the word "victim."

It's as condescending as a pat on the head. A victim never acts; she is always acted upon. A victim never controls; she is always controlled. When you call someone a victim, you call her helpless. Don't misunderstand. I'm not dismissing the threat faced by stalking "victims." Watching behind your back every day is exhausting when it drags on month after month, year after year. I should know. I was a "victim." The difference is—I have never thought of myself as one.

Still, it was never easy. Overcoming years of harassment was a mixed blessing. My ex-boyfriend was my greatest enemy but my greatest teacher. For that I remain grateful.

Some of us may remember our parents scolding us with the hackneyed retort: "What doesn't kill us makes us stronger." Maybe Mom and Dad were right. Those who challenge us the most can be our greatest source of insight. In that spirit, I begin this book—to help, to sympathize and to share.

Describing my daily ritual to a friend one day, I recounted my habits learned through years of vigilance: I carried a stun gun to my car, from my car, to my health club, back home, always aware of what might happen. I kept a gun near my bed. I locked my doors when I stepped outside to mow the lawn, to carry out the trash, to walk down my driveway. I kept my curtains drawn at night and tacked up black cloth around the window edges. I checked my security system frequently. I listened for my driveway alarm late at night. I was alert when the motion detector lights shone brighter.

"That's no way to live," my friend said with a dropped jaw. He was right. I was accustomed to the constant vigilance; my day seemed normal. Surely, all women go about their day in a constant state of watchfulness, I assumed. I grew used to living at full alert. Being cautious was like brushing my teeth. But I was never a victim. I never saw myself as one.

You don't have to be a victim. You may not be able to control what someone else does, but you can control what you do. With a little technical know-how and good instincts, you can stop a stalker in his tracks. You're only a "victim" if you act like one.

You've heard this before, but I'm here to remind you: You are not alone. Still, you may feel like you are. Embarrassed by the unfolding events and trying to maintain a normal life, you will likely hide your private vigilance to retain a sense of normalcy. There were many times I thought to myself: If I ignore him, maybe he will disappear and find another obsession. But this was wishful thinking. He showed no signs of stopping.

You may be in this loop of wishful thinking, too. You may think that maybe he will just go away; you think that if you do what he wants, maybe he'll leave. But statistics suggest that ignoring a stalker is not only futile, it can be deadly.

One in 12 women will be stalked. Ninety percent of stalking victims are female. Over 75 percent of female homicide victims were stalked by the person who killed them. Once considered an unfortunate result of broken relationships, stalking has become the new high-tech crime.

Chapter Two

Katie's Story

Having worked at a newspaper for many years, I've read countless stories about domestic violence, about missing women, and the women who turn up dead. But there was one story that stood out from the rest. It was an article about Katie, a woman who survived harassment and life-threatening encounters from a high-tech stalker. I spoke to Katie, who graciously shared her story. This is her first-person account.

In Katie's words

My boyfriend was the nicest guy in the world. He was charming, very polite, quiet and responsible. If you looked in the dictionary under "Mr. Nice Guy," it seemed like you should see his face. He had everybody fooled.

After a few months, he started calling and text messaging me constantly. One night I had 80 text messages from him. When I confronted him about it, he just laughed it off. When I stopped responding every time he called, I saw more warning signs: He would freak out for no reason. He would ask me where I was on nights I wasn't with him. He would accuse me of lying.

And yet, he would never go anywhere with me, even to family get-togethers. I thought this was weird. I mean, he didn't even want to meet my family for Christmas. He didn't want to do anything, even go to church.

He tried to cut off my communication with the outside world. He changed the passwords on my cellphone and listened to my phone messages. I don't even know how he got my password.

Then he started taking the batteries out of my cordless phone just to get my attention. And he would do it over and over again.

I got tired of it. I put up with him for about six months. I put up with it for three or four months longer than I should have. But he knew how to push my buttons. He knew how to play me.

It didn't get better

He always knew too much about things that happened in my life when he wasn't around. I started thinking something was fishy.

He would constantly accuse me of lying and try to alienate me from some of my friends. So I stopped telling him I was out with friends or I'd hide whom I was with and say something like, "Oh, I'm not talking to her." But he knew. He knew because he was tapping my phone.

"Do you hear that? Do you hear that 'click click?'" a friend asked on the phone one day. "He's taping your phone calls," she insisted. I refused to listen. "He wouldn't do that," I said. I was wrong.

I tried to break up with him. But then he'd be extra nice. He'd come over and do something he knew I wanted him to do. It was a way to slither back into my life. I'd still be mad at him, so he would say, "I'm not so bad, Katie. I just get insecure some-times. That's all. Sometimes I just think you're out to get me." Truth was he was out to get me. I was a sucker. I believed him.

Watching him watch me

It got worse when I tried to cut all ties to him. He started using surveillance equipment, probably because it drove him crazy when he didn't know what I was doing, when I was no longer under his control.

My friend's husband came over one day to investigate. He looked behind the ceiling tiles and found a voice-activated, miniature cassette recorder attached to my phone line. There was another one outside behind the house on my phone box. Other times, he would shut off my phone service by pulling or cutting the lines. He used a lot of wireless, voice-activated recorders. I've got a box full of them. He put one in the box spring of my bed.

I learned to never talk about where I was going on the phone. If the information slipped out, he would show up. So I'd get in my car to call my friends because I figured I was safe in my car. But that's when he started putting recording devices in my car. I found them under my seat and in the back pocket of the driver's seat. They all used cassettes, which he would retrieve and play later. He also got one of those universal remotes to open my garage door and get inside my house. I found out later that was how he was getting into my house. But I didn't figure this out until after I kept changing my locks and wondering how he kept getting inside. When I would leave my house, he would go inside to play the recorders so he could keep up with my whereabouts and personal plans.

He figured out the password on my computer. When I was in my computer room, he would film me with a hidden Web cam. I could tell by the things he said to me.

Once he took a picture of a naked woman and posted it online along with my name, address, phone number. I was always changing my phone number, but he always got the new one, and I still don't know how.

One night, the phone rang when I was in my bedroom with the man who is now my husband. The stalker started yelling at me, "You're a whore! You're a whore!" He threatened to tell my ex-husband, the father of my children, I was a whore and show him all the men I had in my house. He threatened to have my children taken away. He said he knew I was a whore because he could see us in my bedroom. He said he had all the proof he needed to tell my ex-husband and get my kids taken away.

Then he slipped up. He said, "I can see his arms."

That's when Allan and I knew he was filming us. We saw a tiny hole in my TV. We took the TV apart and found a wireless, motion-activated color camera. It turns out he was only 200 feet away with a small television hooked into his car's cigarette lighter recording me in my bedroom through a wireless signal.

I filed for a temporary protective order against him but it was never served because he could never be found. The police tried his workplace, but he had found out, and didn't go back to work. His new job was stalking me.

The police came, an arrest

Luckily, the police arrested him in my yard one day. He was charged with being a "peeping Tom." The judge gave him a 12-month jail sentence. I thought, I'm OK for 12 months. I had a court date for the protective order the following Tuesday. I didn't go through with it because I didn't think I needed it. Now I know I should have gotten the protective order because when he got out four months later, he started stalking again.

As soon as he got out, he called me and said, "Can I come over?" I called the police, but they wouldn't arrest him because I didn't have a protective order. I had a court order—the judge had told him to stay away from me—but the police said that wasn't good enough.

Then the e-mails started. I knew what he was up to, so I prepared. I went to court to get a restraining order and made my house even more secure. I even had my garage doors nailed shut so he couldn't get them open. I thought—finally—he wouldn't be able to get inside.

Then the e-mails started coming. "Do you know how big of a hole a .45 puts in your head? You're about to find out," said one of his e-mails. And he would always threaten to get my kids taken away from me.

That fateful day

A few days later, it seemed like he was leaving me alone. I had peace. I didn't hear from him for 4 or 5 days. At first, I thought the police had served him with the temporary protective order I'd applied for and that's why he was leaving me alone. But they hadn't. Once again, they couldn't find him to deliver it. What was really happening was he was planning his fatal scheme. He planned to shoot me then shoot himself.

The night before, I stayed at my best friend's house. She didn't want me to leave. But I told her I had to go home and change clothes. I said my paycheck is at home. I went home with a male friend, who checked my house. There was no trace of anyone.

Later that day, when I opened the door to go downstairs, I saw him standing there listening. I screamed and slammed the door. That's when he kicked the door open.

So I figure the stalker was there the whole time, hiding. He shot me once. He saw my friend and stepped over my body to go after him. I got up and snuck out the front door. I got shot right under the ribcage where my gall bladder used to be. The bullet went right through me. He shot at my friend, who dove through my bathroom window. But fortunately, my friend got away with a broken arm. Then the stalker shot himself through the neck. The bullet went through his sinuses, between his eyes, came out his hairline and he lived. Now he's in county jail.

Two months after shooting me, the stalker called me on two separate occasions from jail. I called the police, but they wouldn't charge him again, even though it happened after the shooting. They said that the stalker already faced a bunch of charges, so why bother.

We go to trial next month on charges of attempted murder, felony assault, aggravated stalking and use of a stolen firearm.

Chapter Three

High-tech stalking

During the past decade or so, all 50 states have passed anti-stalking laws. Unfortunately, technology helps the stalker stay ahead of the law. Advances in telecommunication have made stalking easier and more insidious. In a University of Cincinnati study, 25 percent of college campus stalking cases involved cyberstalking.

Today, a particularly ominous big brother lurks in a number of new technologies available to the public. Some stalkers have started using a global positioning satellite (GPS), which is small enough to attach to a car. It lets the stalker track your every move without ever getting up from his computer.

Internet ads for tiny surveillance cameras often feature scantily clad women being watched. There's a not-so-subtle sales pitch: "Spy on women. They'll never know."

Cameras, computer programs and identity theft devices often give stalkers access to sophisticated technology the average police officer doesn't understand. Now stalkers with enough computer and technical savvy can turn their habit into a 24/7 obsession.

Cyberstalking

Cyberstalking usually involves strangers who stalk strangers. This is unlike traditional stalking, which commonly involves former intimate partners. Online, a stalker can keep anonymity while using things like AOL's instant messenger (IM), Internet Relay Chat (IRC) rooms and e-mail.

As a result, many states have revised their stalking laws aimed at keeping stalkers out of "close proximity" to widen their reach. But stalking is still seen mainly as a physical crime in which the perpetrator tracks his victim by foot or lurks behind bushes.

The more culture embraces technology, the more it will become a part of our lives and cyberstalking will become synonymous with stalking, not just indicative of a trend among a younger generation.

A growing problem among adolescents is cyber-bullying, and the Internet is an easy way to broadcast anger. Classmates are harassed beyond the playground with online bullying, sometimes found on bulletin boards. Online harassment is easy and anonymous. And it hurts.

Cyber-bullying is used by stalkers, too. It's effective and it's hard for unskilled police officers to trace. A former intimate partner can post nude photographs or a victim's personal information for public view. Several cases of cyberstalking involved the stalker posing as the victim while posting personal information about the victim on the Web.

Gary Dellapenta used the anonymity of the Web to impersonate his victim. He posted rape fantasies on the Web that spurred online readers to action when he included his victim's name, phone number and address. His victim received harassing phone calls and visits to her door by men offering to fulfill her rape fantasy for over a year.

Here's another example: Amy Boyer never knew Liam Youens created a Web site with sick details of his plan to murder her. His obsession grew, and he easily purchased information: Amy Boyer's Social Security number and her place of employment. He got it from an online "information broker," then went to her job and killed her.

Cyberstalking can also ruin your credit or reputation if the stalker uses computer spyware to find out the username and password of a victim's bank account or read private correspondence.

How can you avoid cyberstalking?

- Change your e-mail address and any online chat screen names.
- Do not supply personal information when signing up for new accounts.
- Only use your primary e-mail address when writing to trusted friends and family. Sign up for free e-mail accounts for any or all other communication. Choose an e-mail or screen name that does not identify your name, gender or geography.
- If you join an online discussion, resist the temptation to identify yourself.
- "Google" yourself at www.google.com. Type your name in the search field in the "web," "images" and "groups" directories to see if a stalker has posted any comments or photographs of you online. Google also has an e-mail alert feature that searches keywords—like your name— and then e-mails you the results periodically. Receiving these alerts may warn you if a stalker posts any information about you on the Web.

For staying safe online:

The National Center for Victims of Crime
www.ncvc.org/src

Wired Safety
www.wiredsafety.org

WHOA—Working to Halt Online Abuse
www.haltabuse.org

Chapter Four

The lowdown on the low-tech

Whether or not a stalker uses new technology, most still stalk with low-tech predictability. Expect them to do one or all of the following:

- Leave notes or presents at your door
- Call your friends and family to get their support
- Try to obtain your bank records or other financial statements
- Rummage through your trash
- Look through your windows
- Talk to your co-workers
- Follow you
- Threaten physical violence
- Break into your home
- Vandalize your property
- Kill or threaten your pet
- Threaten suicide

Given these predictabilities, what should you do?

Disengage

The day I told my ex-boyfriend he was no longer welcome back into my home you could hear the panic in his voice. Before I called him I had taken all of his belongings that were in my house and put them in storage. "Put my stuff back," he said, holding back his anger. "No," I replied. My breakup was scripted to be short. There was no longer any room for discussion. I knew that emotions only made the water murky, a lesson I would soon learn when my resolve faltered.

Then, midstream into the talk, he did an about-face: "Never mind. I won't be coming back. What's the point? Please…take care of my cat…my things. I'm sorry. I won't be needing them anymore," he said in heavy gasping breaths. I couldn't gauge whether this was genuine emotion. Frightened by his tone, I reached out with a feeble offer. "Come back and let's talk. I mean, you aren't welcome back here, but don't do anything stupid. It's not worth it." What I regarded as help, he regarded as an open invitation to track me down. In subsequent legal proceedings, he called it "an invitation."

A controlling person who stalks takes the tiniest hint of friendly behavior as an open invitation. So don't break from the script. Don't fall for emotional pleas. If someone threatens suicide, call the police but do not act as savior. To this day I recognize my ex-boyfriend's suicide threat as what I instinctually knew at the time but ignored—bogus. He feigned emotions to elicit emotions from me.

When I disengaged, he did what most stalkers do. He moved on to my friends and family and tried to influence them to influence me. His tactical assaults did not succeed. So he expanded his attack to my neighbors. When I moved, he got cozy with my neighbors, telling them we were married, that he lived with me, while all the while "helping" the community with zoning issues. This allowed him excusable access to my neighborhood to better watch me under the guise of helping the community.

Engaging a stalker is always a bad idea. Even negative communication is communication for a stalker, and that is what he wants, negative or not. Cease all communication. What you're saying isn't what a stalker hears anyway.

What you say	What a stalker hears
Don't hurt yourself; let's talk	She wants to see me
I want some time alone	She wants to see me in a few days
Leave me alone	She must want to see me; otherwise, she wouldn't be talking to me.
Black	White
No	Maybe

Get the picture? It doesn't matter what you say, a stalker will hear what he wants. Telling him one more time isn't going to change that.

- **Disengage.** Stop all communication with a stalker. This includes e-mail, phone calls, messages through friends, cellphone text messages and smoke signals. Disengage completely and without remorse. Do not extend grace periods or other misguided kindnesses. Kindness is only regarded as weakness, and weakness equates to opportunity.

File a TPO—Temporary Protective Order

On good advice from a friend, I stayed at a hotel after breaking it off with my ex-boyfriend. His reaction was suspicious, and I knew he'd be coming straight for me. When I returned the next day, the back door was ajar. I called the police. The night before, he had broken into my home, disabled my security system and deleted files from my computer. I found a photograph of a male friend on my refrigerator door, torn at the nape of my friend's neck, decapitating him. The next day, I went to the courthouse to file for a temporary protective order (TPO), also known as a restraining order.

I visited the victim's assistance office at my county's courthouse, looking for help. I was told I couldn't file for a TPO unless there was a warrant out for my ex-boyfriend's arrest. I couldn't get a warrant for his arrest because no one saw him enter my home. I left only to find out later that the woman at the courthouse had given me misinformation. I got a TPO a month later after an advocate at a battered women's shelter took me through the maze of paperwork. If you doubt the assistance of government workers, don't hesitate to get a second opinion from a women's shelter or other organizations that specialize in helping women. Too often, government workers are misinformed.

Some states require that a direct threat be verbalized or actualized before they will issue a TPO. This is unfortunate since many stalkers only insinuate a threat with "harmless" ploys designed to intimidate. People should have the right to live without worrying about a stalker tracking them down, regardless of whether a threat is direct or implied.

A TPO orders someone to stay away from a victim for a set distance, usually 100 feet from the person or that person's property. The accused may not contact the defendant through letters, e-mail, phone calls or third parties. When you first apply for a TPO, it only lasts for 30 days until the hearing, and is not official until the accused is served and is ordered to attend the hearing. If your application for a TPO is granted it usually lasts for 6 months to a year. If the stalking persists, you can file for a permanent order, which lasts for life.

There is debate about TPOs as a deterrent. Some argue that it is just a piece of paper. It is. The last I looked at mine, it seemed to be typed on your standard 8 1/2-by-11 paper. Yes, a TPO is just a piece of paper, but it is a piece of paper that shows law enforcement, and maybe the stalker, you are serious. Without a paper trail, your entreaties will have less significance in the eyes of a judge or jury. Without a TPO, police can't arrest a stalker for breaking a TPO. Your story will just be white noise. Failing to file for a TPO could indicate you don't take the situation seriously, so neither will the law.

On the other hand, some say TPOs instigate violence, especially if there was past physical violence. The problem with this argument is that it blames the person being stalked by implying that if a victim hadn't filed for a TPO, the stalker would have had no cause to become violent. But victims aren't responsible for the mental stability of stalkers and shouldn't have to just wait and hope that someday the craziness will end.

In his book, "The Gift of Fear," Gavin de Becker makes an interesting point in support of this argument. It is better to get a stalker convicted of other crimes, he argues, than for violating a temporary protective order (TPO). Battery, trespass and peeping Tom are crimes against the state, whereas violating a TPO is a crime against a person. Stalkers love control. When a victim files a TPO, she is taking away a stalker's control, which is why de Becker believes murder-suicides often are prompted when a victim fights back.

I have first-hand experience with the shortcomings of stalking laws. It wasn't the aggravated stalking charges that went to trial. It was the felony peeping Tom and the misdemeanor criminal trespass charges. And now I have a permanent protective order (PPO) and he is not allowed to come back after serving his sentence and stalk me yet again.

At no time did I want to call the police if he violated the TPO. I was hoping he wouldn't give me reason to, that he would just disappear, go on with his life. But someone so intent on control doesn't give up easily. It takes firm legal intervention.

Many victims fail to file for a TPO when the stalking persists, even if physically threatened. Studies show many stalking incidents go unreported. Some think the situation will get better. It rarely does. If a stalker is breaking into your home, harassing your friends, threatening violence or interfering with your daily life, it may be time to file for a TPO. Listen to your instincts. A TPO is not a mark that will start or add to a criminal record. Stalking only becomes a crime if someone breaks a TPO.

- **Disengage**
- **File for a TPO**—if the stalking persists, is unduly invasive or potentially violent, file for a TPO. If you are being stalked by an intimate partner with a history of physical violence, use your best judgment. And remember: Bring a copy of your TPO with you wherever you go. You'll need it to incite action if the order is violated.

Keep a detailed log

I never thought I would be sitting here writing down all the events two years after I ended the relationship. My expandable folder is pregnant with the drama that was my life, detailed in police reports and legal proceedings. It has come in handy. You should keep a log of every event, even if you cannot obtain a police report about it. The timeline of events can blur over time, and the details fade in your memory because you want to forget.

I remember rattling off the long list of stalking incidents for a state prosecutor. A few days later, I ran across a police report I had filed away regarding the night police found my ex-boyfriend's car on my property. The police could not find him that night, so they left. I couldn't recall this incident when talking to the prosecutor but because I asked for a police report, I had a record of it as a reminder.

Two years after we broke up, my ex-boyfriend faced three charges: a misdemeanor charge of criminal trespass, a felony charge of peeping Tom, and a felony charge of aggravated stalking. When I prepared for court, it was the detail in my log that made my case stronger against him.

Your log should contain at least the first four things listed here:

o   Date
o   Time
o   Description
o   Observations
o   Police report number
o   Police officer's name
o   Witnesses' names and phone numbers

If you file a police report, you should always go to the courthouse and get a copy for your files. Read the report and make sure it is accurate. Days turn into months, and months turn into years. Logging the events will help you remember the facts, if you should find yourself in court. Cases can take years to go to trial, and with unpleasant incidents you would just as soon forget. It is best to keep a log.

- **Disengage**
- **File for a TPO**

- **Keep a detailed log**. Keep a record of the dates with a detailed description of the events.

Save the evidence

First came the e-mails and phone calls, all apologetic and clearly manipulative. Later came the presents and letters taped to my door and trashcan. Don't be fooled by the feigned sentiments. Stalkers refuse to use the US Postal Service for good reason: They can't stalk you through a postal worker. Taping things to your door or dropping off boxes on your porch are clear signs they lurk. It is a subtle sign that they are in control. Keep the evidence. Do not return the gifts or acknowledge them. This only communicates to a stalker that you are communicating with him. It doesn't matter what kind of communication—negative or positive—it is communication.

A letter taped to my trashcan proved invaluable when I sought a permanent restraining order. Skulking around taping notes to garbage cans is a sign of a stalker, not someone who clearly knows the convenient benefits of postage.

- **Disengage**
- **File for a TPO**
- **Keep a detailed log**
- **Save the evidence**. Do not cash any checks (unless they are for child support) or delete any e-mails or throw away any notes a stalker leaves you. If you have a TPO, communication of any kind violates the order.

Change your personal account information

It became evident the relationship had to end. He was unemployed, living in my home, and a job wasn't imminent. The relationship was in a downward spiral. It had to end, but I knew this would be difficult. This kept me paralyzed for months, unable to make the break.

He used my checking account. He knew my credit card numbers and had access to all of my personal information. I orchestrated his departure carefully as his anger escalated with every passing month.

I closed my bank accounts and credit card accounts to open new ones with account numbers he didn't know. But I forgot about my online accounts, which gave easy access to personal information.

My ex-boyfriend was a computer hacker, making him a technical pro most people won't encounter. But even a novice can learn to use a hacker program. Although I couldn't prove it, my computer acted strangely for months until it finally stopped working. Before my computer self-combusted, my ex-boyfriend hacked into two dating sites I had used. He sent an e-mail to a man I had communicated with on one of the dating sites that was offensive. I found my profile on another dating site rewritten the next day. It is likely my ex-boyfriend used a hacker program that logged all of my keystrokes, then sent this list to himself as an e-mail attachment. Changing my usernames and passwords would not have solved the problem unless I had used a different computer to change my usernames and passwords.

- **Disengage**
- **File for a TPO**
- **Keep a detailed log**
- **Save the evidence**
- **Change account information.** Close your checking accounts, savings accounts and credit card accounts. Open new ones. Change your usernames and passwords on all online accounts. Do not use frequently used phrases or birthdates for usernames and passwords.

Install blinds and curtains

Sounds simple. Yet I didn't worry about it because I didn't think my ex-boyfriend would skulk around at night peeping into my windows. That is, until around midnight one summer night.

I was at my computer typing away, my curtains wide open. My cat's eyes jolted with sudden intensity looking into the black of night. My cat had done this before, in the same room, on many occasions. Always, I had looked out the window and never saw a thing. But this time was different. My mother had visited two weeks before and cut back the shrubs. This allowed me to see a reflection—a tiny camera on an extendable arm peering at me.

I wanted to jump back and scream. Instead, I went back to my computer, waited a few minutes, then walked into the hall-way to call 911. Much to my alarm, it took the police 45 min-utes—after repeated phone calls—to arrive. In the meantime, I put on a show. I sat in my office and surfed dating Web sites because I knew this would keep his attention. I didn't want to tip him off that I knew, so I didn't look out the window. Every so often, I lifted up my cat to see if it still saw the camera. It did. I knew I had a captive audience.

When the police finally arrived, they found his car boldly parked in the middle of my driveway. I lived on 12 acres in a forest. There were plenty of places to hide. I was lucky that night. As one police officer took my statement, another looked outside with a flashlight. When he turned off the flashlight, the leaves rustled as my ex-boyfriend tried to flee. He was caught and arrested.

In hindsight, I should have been more cautious. But I had a full security system. What I didn't take into account was why someone would peer into my window. For my ex-boyfriend, it wasn't about seeing me in my pajamas, it was about watching me on my computer. Who was I writing? What account was I logging into? Save yourself the drama. Make your living space private and secure.

- **Disengage**
- **File for a TPO**
- **Keep a detailed log**
- **Save the evidence**
- **Change account information**
- **Cover all windows and doors.** Use blinds or opaque curtains. You can buy instant blinds at a hardware store for around $5. They tape right on and last forever.

Protect your credit

Knowing the high-tech skills that my ex-boyfriend could use against my personal finances, I slept better at night knowing my credit was protected. You can put a temporary credit fraud alert on your credit within minutes. Just call one of the three credit agencies: Equifax, TransUnion or Experion. Your one call will be automatically reported to the other two agencies. Or, be extra safe and call all three.

Equifax: 800-525-6285
Experian: 888-397-3742
Transunion: 800-680-7289

Credit agencies know identity theft is growing and fraud alerts are easier to activate 24/7—and you can do it by punching in numbers on your phone's keypad. A temporary fraud alert lasts around six months. If someone opens a credit line or tries to borrow money based on your credit, the credit agencies are required to call you for authorization.

After adding the temporary fraud alert, I signed up to have Equifax alert me within 24 hours of any changes to my credit report. It cost $9.95 a month. You might choose another service. Just make sure it's a reputable company.

You also should stop all the credit card offers filling your mailbox. You don't want anyone stealing and filling out a credit application in your name. To stop credit card offers, call: 1-888-5 OPT OUT

- **Disengage**
- **File for a TPO**
- **Keep a detailed log**
- **Save the evidence**
- **Change account information**
- **Cover all windows and doors**
- **Protect your credit.** (Equifax and Privacy Guard both charge around $9.95 a month).

Protect your mail

Stalkers hate using postage but love your unattended mail. They can retrieve your account numbers and other personal information by visiting your mailbox while you're at work, and even when you're at home. Invest in a post office box to route all your mail to a secure location. You don't want to give a stalker your new account numbers.

Renting a post office box only costs around $40 a year. I had all my mail forwarded to a post office box. What I didn't plan on was how adeptly my ex-boyfriend circumvented my plan. When he broke into my home, he found the number of my post office box written down. He was quick to rush to the same post office and rent one, too. He convinced the mail distributor we were married and that any mail with my name on it, but with his address, should be routed to his mailbox just a few paces away.

Two months later, I learned about this conversation after I received his bill in my postal box. When I spoke to the mail distributor, she told me how my "husband" had explained to her where to direct any mail that had my name on it but his address. For two months, my cellphone bills were going to his box. He had access to my incoming and outgoing cellphone calls for months before I found out.

- **Disengage**
- **File for a TPO**
- **Keep a detailed log**
- **Save the evidence**
- **Change account information**
- **Cover all windows and doors**
- **Protect your credit**
- **Protect your mail.** Be sure to shred your old bills and documents (or burn them). And don't send mail by leaving it in your mailbox for a postal carrier to pick up. Identity theft criminals scan neighborhoods in search of an upright red flag on a mailbox.

Protect your documents

One day at work, the phone rang. "Your husband just left our office, and I forgot to tell him…," a voice of concern said. It was the secretary for the attorney handling my home closing.

"My husband?" I replied.

"He walked out and your phone number was the one I found in our files."

I was lucky she called that day. My ex-boyfriend had convinced the secretary we were married. Never mind that we didn't have the same last name or that he wasn't on any of my mortgage documents. This legal secretary nearly handed over my private information after simply hearing the story he spun about a flood destroying the title to "our" home. I was aghast. Although you can do little to avoid other people foolishly disclosing your personal information, you can protect what is in your possession. This is why I suggest getting a safe deposit box for keeping your valuables and documents.

- **Disengage**
- **File for a TPO**
- **Keep a detailed log**
- **Save the evidence**
- **Change account information**
- **Cover all windows and doors**
- **Protect your credit**
- **Protect your mail**
- **Protect your documents.** They might include: home title, deeds, other legal agreements or stock certificates.

Pay attention to your gut

I had a feeling—a bad feeling—as I drove up the gravel road past my home one moonless night. The only neighbors I had were a retired couple 1,000 feet away. When I boldly traveled up past my home, I was not surprised to find his van parked on the side of the road. I was tempted to block his car so he couldn't escape. I called 911, but was told I couldn't block him in; it was against the law. The irony. So I stayed in my car, with the doors locked. He emerged from the woods with a flashlight and shined it in my windows. It was a lame attempt at intimidation. I was lucky he wasn't carrying a weapon. He walked back to his van, started it, and veered toward me, barely missing my car and sped off. The police arrived. Late. As usual. I filed my sixth police report.

I don't recommend the bold manner in which I confronted my ex-boyfriend. I took my chances. But I had had enough. I was tired of hiding, of hearing people tell me to sell my home, to move away, to change my life. I wanted my life back, and I was going to stand my ground. I suggest you make your own decision, the one that is best for you.

- **Disengage**
- **File for a TPO**
- **Keep a detailed log**
- **Save the evidence**
- **Change account information**
- **Cover all windows and doors**
- **Protect your credit**
- **Protect your mail**
- **Pay attention to your instinct**. It's amazing what our instincts tell us. Unfortunately, most of the time we aren't listening.

Demand police reports

When my ex-boyfriend broke into my home after our break up, the officer who arrived could not have been more disinterested. There was no proof my ex-boyfriend had broken in. To the officer, it was just another "domestic dispute." But I demanded a police report. Later, the crawlspace alarm was disconnected in my second home. The officer who arrived had the same attitude. I did meet some sympathetic officers in my three-year ordeal, but they were few and far between.

I'll stop short of making Krispy Kreme jokes and simply say that filling out paperwork is a task some police officers would rather avoid. If there is no proof of a crime, request a police report, and get the number for the report before the officer leaves. It is your right. Then go to your county courthouse with the police report number to get the report. Officers sometimes record the events differently than they occurred. If you end up back in court, you want the report to reflect your testimony. If an officer refuses to modify a report that contains an error, have your lawyer call. Without documented proof of an event, your word is just your word. Document, document, document.

- **Disengage**
- **File for a TPO**
- **Keep a detailed log**
- **Save the evidence**
- **Change account information**
- **Cover all windows and doors**
- **Protect your credit**
- **Protect your mail**
- **Pay attention to your gut**
- **Demand police reports.** A police report may not prove anything else in court, but it proves you are serious.

Disconnect any joint services

Do as I say, not as I do. I learned the hard way. Despite advice to cut him off completely, I let my ex-boyfriend remain on my cellphone account so he could continue to conduct business. I thought this was overwhelmingly nice of me. But, it was just very stupid. He offered to pay the cellphone bill "for life" if he could stay on the account. I declined. Instead, I gave him a deadline for when he must quit using it. He phoned a relative, who felt moved to intervene on my ex-boyfriend's behalf. I gave him more time on my cellphone account. But keeping him on my account hurt me in two ways:

1) During the TPO hearing, he accused me of using his credit card to pay my bill. Actually, he paid the bill, an arrangement he had set up.

2) He gained control of my cellphone account and had the bills for it mailed to his post office box. The bills listed every phone number going in and out of my cellphone, making it easy for him to harass my family and friends.

Hindsight is 20/20 and I must have been blind. Cellphone records are a fertile source for stalkers. He also set up an account online, making it easy to access my records. Check to see whether your accounts are being accessed online. If you haven't set up an account, you may want to log in and set a password so a stalker doesn't.

- **Disengage**
- **File for a TPO**
- **Keep a detailed log**
- **Save the evidence**
- **Change account information**
- **Cover all windows and doors**
- **Protect your credit**
- **Protect your mail**
- **Pay attention to your gut**
- **Demand police reports**
- **Disconnect any joint services.** I learned the hard way. I kept him on my cellphone and paid a big price.

Change your patterns

I went to lunch with a co-worker one sunny day and we sat next to a large window facing the street. We were well into work banter when I looked up and saw my ex-boyfriend drive by with a big smile. I was predictable enough to leave for lunch at the same time from the same door every weekday. And he was watching. Just because you don't see a stalker, doesn't mean a stalker isn't lurking; it just means you aren't aware.

Don't let a stalker know your next move. Stalkers depend on predictability. We all have patterns. You may walk to your car at the same time, by the same route, every day. But you should mix it up a little and stay alert. And check your rear-view mirror frequently.

- **Disengage**
- **File for a TPO**
- **Keep a detailed log**
- **Save the evidence**
- **Change account information**
- **Cover all windows and doors**
- **Protect your credit**
- **Protect your mail**
- **Pay attention to your gut**
- **Demand police reports**
- **Disconnect any joint services**
- **Change your patterns.** "Every move you make, every step you take, I'll be watching you".—The Police

Don't sympathize

Eighteen months of harassment took its toll. My ex-boyfriend kept dragging me through civil courts on baseless claims, which threatened the few assets I had left. He broke into my home and disarmed my alarm system—twice. He phoned my family and friends, insinuated himself into my neighborhood and workplace. He made my every move one of caution. But I still showed compassion. When the cops arrested him one night, I was given a choice.

1) Let my ex-boyfriend leave with a warning to stay off of my property.

2) Press charges of peeping Tom, a felony. A court date would be set about 30 days later, and the police would escort him off my property immediately.

3) My third choice was the same as the second choice except my ex-boyfriend would be thrown in jail for a night and his car impounded.

The first choice wasn't enough of a deterrent after 18 months of harassment. I chose the second option. I look back and wonder why. I should have put him in jail even if it was only for a few hours. It would have made more of an impression. Instead, I made a choice he might see as weak and even affectionate. I believe my choice was based on misguided pity for a man violating my life and privacy, a man who was suing me, causing me serious financial problems, and stalking me relentlessly. It's funny how turned around people get, when it comes to spouses or partners. If a stranger were doing this, we wouldn't be compassionate. Jail makes an impression. There are no fuzzy lines. Sympathy only works to your disadvantage.

- Disengage
- File for a TPO
- Keep a detailed log
- Save the evidence
- Change account information
- Cover all windows and doors
- Protect your credit
- Protect your mail
- Pay attention to your gut
- Demand police reports
- Disconnect any joint services
- Change your patterns

- **Don't sympathize.** Show concern for stray animals, not someone who uses intimidation and manipulation to control you.

Get away

The first few weeks after a breakup with an aggressive partner are the most dangerous. Get to a safe place—like a hotel or a friend's home—during this vulnerable time, especially the first few days. I don't suggest running away, unless there is a history of physical violence. For the first few days find a hotel or friend's home in which to stay.

I often found solace in hotel rooms. I stayed in a hotel room one night when I knew my ex-boyfriend would be pounding on my door. It was one of the most relaxing nights I'd ever had. The luxury of being far from the drama of the courtroom and being able to quit looking over my shoulder has given me many nights of sorely needed respite. The stress of being stalked can wear you down in subtle ways that you may not even recognize until the quiet of anonymity lulls you into a night's safe haven.

- **Disengage**
- **File for a TPO**
- **Keep a detailed log**
- **Save the evidence**
- **Change account information**
- **Cover all windows and doors**
- **Protect your credit**
- **Protect your mail**
- **Pay attention to your gut**
- **Demand police reports**
- **Disconnect any joint services**
- **Change your patterns**

- **Don't sympathize**
- **Get away.** If even for one night. The first few weeks are the most dangerous when breaking up with potentially violent partners.

More Resources:

Stalking Victims Sanctuary
www.stalkingvictims.com

An Abuse, Rape, Domestic Violence and Resource Collection
www.aardvarc.org

Chapter Five

What you should buy

Even if no physical violence has occurred, you never know what a stalker will do next. Implied threats wind up being linked to violent acts more than overt threats do. Physical violence often leads to more physical violence. But don't count on past behavior to predict future behavior. Victims of violence can't predict what will happen next, because most people ignore the signs and hope for the best. Be smart and prepare for the worst.

LOW-TECH SELF PROTECTION

Whistle ($1–$3)

Maybe you've seen the well-polished whistles in women's boutiques touting female empowerment. A less expensive one works the same way. A whistle may not protect you, but in a public place it may scare away an attacker, when you're too afraid to scream for help. Place it on your keychain for easy access when opening doors to your home and car.

Mace or pepper spray ($10–$30)

Upgrade to a Mace or pepper spray keychain for around $10. Then walk to your car or door with extra peace of mind. I bought Mace that fits into a purse at the Cop Shop, a store that sells self-defense items to police officers. Mace is one of the least expensive weapons you can use at a safe distance from an attacker. Just make sure the wind isn't blowing in your direction.

Knife ($20+)

Don't use a knife unless you've studied martial arts. There is a good chance it will be taken from you.

HIGH-TECH SELF PROTECTION

Stun gun ($40–$100)

Stun guns immobilize an attacker, but you need to be within arm's length, and in harm's way, to use one. If you aren't certain you can keep a hold of it, don't buy one. Mace may be a better option. I bought a foot-long stun gun at a police supply store. It was a standard stun gun that crackled when the two points of electricity met in the middle. Or you might buy a "flying taser" gun, which allows up to 20 feet between you and an attacker. It can be used only once before you must install a new gas cartridge.

If you want the element of surprise, you could try a "decoy" stun gun, which is disguised as an umbrella or other household item. For interactive details on how a stun gun works and which one you should buy visit: electronics.howstuffworks.com/stun-gun1.htm

Guns ($200–$800)

Once I realized a stun gun would do me little good since my ex-boyfriend was a martial arts expert, I visited a gun shop to find out how comfortable I'd feel having a gun in my home. Be sure to try out many types of guns at a shooting range with gun rentals before buying. If you do purchase a gun, know how to use it. Take a class: some cater to women.

A popular brand among women is the RUGER SP101 double-action revolver. It's compact and comfortably fits a woman's hand, and fires with little recoil. I recommend double-action revolvers because they require a relatively long pull of the trigger. Guns with hammer spurs that are cocked back before pulling a trigger are easier to fire than double-action revolvers. Double-action revolvers are harder to shoot, which means it is less likely to make a mistake. You want to make sure when you pull the trigger, you really mean it.

If you need to carry a gun with you, a double-action revolver is more practical than guns with hammer spurs, which can get caught on fabric and thus increase the chance of accidentally going off.

Installing a "hair trigger" on your gun makes pulling the trigger easier, but it also makes accidents a greater likelihood. Check your local concealed-weapons permit laws before carrying a weapon. In most cases, obtaining a concealed-weapons permit can take six to eight weeks.

And remember: You should feel comfortable with the gun you buy. So understand what you're buying and how to use it.

Laws may vary by state and circumstance, but when it comes to defending yourself with a gun if your home is invaded, there is little doubt you are acting in self-defense. A final, ominous note: Never buy a gun unless you're certain you can use it in self-defense. If you don't use it, it can be used against you.

LOW-TECH SECURITY

You don't have a lot of money to spend. You need to protect yourself. There are low-cost, low-tech options you should consider:

New locks ($50–$300)

So you never lived together? You think there is no need to change your locks? You may be right. But an intimate partner who stalks is someone who would likely secure a way into your life, emotionally and physically, long before you break up.

I changed the locks on the doors of my home. But I forgot to replace the padlock to the crawlspace and the lock that secured my lawnmower. My ex-boyfriend saw this as an opportunity. He broke into my home through the crawlspace. Two months later, I found him mowing my lawn!

Be two steps ahead of a stalker and pinpoint all means of access. Hiring a locksmith to rekey existing locks costs less than buying new locks, but make sure any doors with glass windows have double-key locks (locks on both sides). An intruder cannot break the window and simply turn the deadbolt from the other side if you have double-key locks. Also make sure you have deadbolts on all outside doors. Doorknobs with privacy locks fitted in its knob offer little protection. And that's ditto for hollow doors. Buy a steel or solid wood door that someone can't kick down.

Paper shredder ($30–$60)

Stalkers love any bit of evidence they can gather about your life, your communication and your financial affairs. Due to recent laws, most credit card receipts only print out the last four digits of your credit card numbers, but some still print out your entire credit card number on the receipt. Receipts have dates and times that reveal where you go and when. A Barnes & Noble receipt may seem insignificant to you, but to a stalker, it places you in a particular place at a particular time. Lists and notes to yourself also provide a wealth of information about your activities and recent purchases. Stalkers are looking for patterns. Buy a paper shredder. Don't give a stalker a shred of evidence.

Doorstop alarm ($10)

This battery-operated device fits under a closed door and sounds an alarm if the door opens. Place one under all main entrances, including the door to your bedroom.

Dial *57 (call trace)

Ask your phone company whether it offers a call tracing service. If you are receiving unwanted phone calls, you can trace a call by picking up the receiver after the call and dialing *57. This sends a call trace signal to the annoyance call center. If the annoyance call center logs calls from this line repeatedly, a letter is sent to the offender's address. Most telephone companies offer this free of charge if you have an unlimited usage plan. If you don't, it will cost around $3.50 every time you trace a call. Keep in mind that this feature is limited. If a phone number does not show up in the caller ID window, the call probably cannot be traced.

HIGH-TECH SECURITY

High-tech devices have become commonplace, and might be more affordable than you think. You don't need every gadget on the market, but a few of the lower cost alternatives may fit your needs.

Wireless video camera with motion detector ($100–$300)

A video camera would have tipped me off to the mischief going on in my driveway in the wee hours of the night. One night the renewal tag on my license was stripped off. Two days later, I found the tag taped back on when I returned to my car after exiting the Department of Motor Vehicles with its replacement.

Another day, my lawnmower stopped working. Diagnosis from the service center was water in the tank. And then there was the time a car tire went flat, with a nail lodged deep in its tread. Paranoia? It's doubtful that water got in my lawnmower gas line; the lawnmower was kept indoors. The gas can was kept outdoors in the carport, safe and dry, but easily accessible to anyone lurking around at night.

My video camera purchase was an inexpensive alternative to hiring a security company to install cameras. Two motion detectors, a receiver and two wireless cameras set me back $150, compared with the thousands of dollars a security company would have charged to install cameras.

Most wireless video setups you can buy online come with at least one camera, a receiver and a motion detector. The motion detector is a small battery-powered device. When motion is detected, a signal is sent to the camera. You need a VCR to attach the camera's sensors, which means the VCR needs to be within range of the wireless devices to work. The camera then sends a signal to the receiver, which turns on the VCR to record the motion.

Besides installation, the main setup difference between a professionally installed camera and one purchased online is the quality of the picture. Not all VCRs connected to wireless cameras provide a date and time on the recorded image. A time stamp makes evidence more convincing in court.

Place a camera in each key location you think an intruder may target, such as your garage, crawlspace door and basement windows. Unless you buy a more expensive camera with night vision, you will need to keep the area well-lit with a contractor's lamp you can buy at hardware store for around $20.

Time-date generator ($70–$80)

If you need to time stamp any video source, a time-date generator will imprint your evidence with the exact time and day.

Driveway alarm ($70–$90)

By far my best purchase was a driveway alarm called The Reporter. I bought it at a spy shop, then realized I could get it online with a lot less hassle at www.smarthome.com. It is a wireless motion detector that works up to 1,000 feet away. Some ads claim driveway alarms work at distances greater than they really do and fail to mention that terrain and trees can block the signal. But The Reporter worked true to its claims, active for 600 feet through dense forest.

A driveway alarm is a wireless, battery-operated device that you stick on a tree near your driveway (or anywhere). They claim to detect only humans and motor vehicles. That's how it worked for me. Wild animals never set it off.

You place the receiver in your house and it beeps when a car or person walking by sets if off. It worked wonders for me in a rural area, but you could just as easily use it in your basement, garage, or carport in town.

Motion detector unit ($50–$60)

You may be more interested in monitoring a gate or mailbox. Battery-operated motion detectors connect to an object and send wireless signals inside your house to your receiver, warning you when a door or mailbox is opened. (This item is found at smarthome.com, item 7466. Alternatives at this site include the Voice Alert System, item 7138).

Cellphone equipped with camera ($100+)

When my ex-boyfriend marched up to my car and shined a flashlight at me, I used my cellphone to call 911. The police arrived late. I had no proof he had done anything. It was another "he said, she said." A cellphone camera would have been helpful. Recently, a man was convicted of indecent exposure after a woman used a cellphone to catch him in the act. Think about it. If an assailant comes near you, a quick shot of him, or his car, is potential evidence. Try to immediately e-mail the image to yourself via your cellphone in case the stalker grabs hold of your phone and runs away with the evidence. A cellphone that takes photos is like having two self-protection devices in one. If you can't buy a cellphone with this feature, at least have a regular cellphone. It gives you access to immediate help. And be sure to keep a cellphone charger in your car.

Motion detector floodlights ($50)

Living on acreage afforded me the luxury of not worrying about curtains or shades on all windows. But at night, the lights lit my house like a stage for an audience of one, as I would later find out, because he frequently skulked around my property at night and watched for hours.

Floodlights would have been a good idea because they prohibit visibility. I recommend security lights that shine brighter when they detect motion because they act as a warning, not just a deterrent.

Security system ($500+)

A full security system is expensive but gives extra peace of mind. I had a full security system. An alarm would go off of any window or door if opened. But my ex-boyfriend knew a lot about electronics. He broke into my first home and disabled the entire system. He broke into my second home and disabled my crawlspace sensor. Even so, it's usually hard for a stalker to beat a security system.

A beep chimes throughout the house when any alarmed door or window is opened. Even when the alarm system is turned off, you'll know when someone enters your home. If the alarm is turned on, an alarm will sound. If you do not answer the phone number listed with your security company when your alarm goes off, the police will be called to your home. I even had a cellphone backup system so that if the phone lines were cut, the alarm system would still call for help. I also had motion detectors in my basement, laundry room and crawlspace. Sensitivity varies among motion detectors. Some detect motion through walls; others ignore domestic animals.

An alarm system should have at least one keypad near each major entrance. The keypad has a panic button you can push if an intruder shows up. My house had one at the front door, one in my bedroom and one in the basement. I recommend having one in your bedroom as well as one in your entryway. The keypads also come with "hostage codes." Say you walk into your house and an intruder comes in from behind you, forcing his way inside, and orders you to turn off your alarm system. What you can do instead is key in a "hostage code," which turns off the alarm but signals the alarm call center and police.

If you can't afford a full security system, try non-tech alternatives. Nails driven into a window frame deter break-ins. Just make sure you have a backup route to exit your place in case of a fire.

Small video cameras and motion detectors can be purchased on the Internet for use in and around your home. The only problem with these low-cost alternatives is they can't trigger a call to the police, in the event an intruder gets to you before you get to a phone.

Check your security system every week to make sure it is working. One night, my alarm detected motion in my basement, triggering the alarm at 5 a.m. The police came but couldn't find a prowler. A few days later, I checked my alarm system and found that the crawlspace sensor didn't work. My alarm company sent a technician, who verified the wires to my crawlspace door had been rewired. I asked the technician to wait for the police to include it as testimony in a police report. Imagine if I didn't have an alarm system on that night. What would have happened if he broke in while I was sleeping?

Make a quick call to the alarm service call center before you do a weekly test so it isn't mistaken for a signal of real intruders. When choosing an alarm company, I recommend one with a month-by-month plan. Large security companies often require long contracts.

I also recommend a security system with cellphone backup. If your phone lines are cut, the alarm will still work. Cellphone backups cost anywhere from $200–$300. Totally wireless security systems are popping up as an alternative you may want to consider. You can skip the land line altogether and opt for a cellphone system instead.

Finally, an important note from my experience: Make sure the bill to the security system is in your name. Security companies consider the name on the account the owner of the security system and will comply with requests only from the person who signed the contract.

Dog-barking alarm with wireless motion detector (around $100)

One alternative cheaper than a full security system is a dog-barking alarm triggered by a motion detector. To be most effective, more than one wireless motion detector should be used with it. You want all entryways covered.

Automatic emergency dialer (around $120)

What if you don't have a security system and don't have time to call police when someone bursts in? You might want a one-touch emergency dialer. It calls for help and plays your prerecorded message giving your location. The device has multiple buttons, so it can alert police, an ambulance or the fire department. This is another smarthome.com device.

Night vision camera ($400–$800+)

Night vision cameras record clear images in the dark. Digital night vision cameras can record without the green hue that distorts cheaper night vision images. I only recommend a night vision camera for highly trafficked areas or other areas an intruder is most likely to target. As with all cameras, you can save money by recording only when motion is detected. Make sure it has a time stamp, if you want to play the recording in court.

Fake surveillance camera (around $30)

Sometimes you don't have to spend a lot. A fake video camera can be a powerful deterrent to the untrained eye. You can't record criminal behavior, but you may prevent it.

Spy sunglasses (around $40)

If you want your sunglasses to work like your car's rear view mirror, try these on for size. Rarely do we turn around and look when we are determined to reach our next destination. But in your haste to be on time, you may forfeit your privacy. The sunglasses might give you an edge.

Bug detectors ($200–$1,500)

Phone taps and other bugging devices usually are illegal in the U.S. unless authorized by a court. But that doesn't mean stalkers can't get such devices. How can you check your house? Phone taps, video surveillance and audio bugs can be detected with counter-surveillance devices that run around $200. They come in many forms. There's an audio bug detector masquerading as a clock radio that shuts off the clock's LCD time display if someone walks in with an audio bug, for example. But most counter surveillance devices must be within six to eight feet of the tapping device before a signal is triggered.

We've all seen cop shows with a crime-scene investigation team scanning the room for evidence. There is usually one cop who waves a small wand around phones and furniture. This is known as a "professional sweep." These baton-like devices cost around $500. I found a less expensive option, the RF Signal Detector, at smarthome.com for around $80. If you want to scan for all types of surveillance—a phone tap, audio bug and video camera—you can buy a professional kit at a security store for around $1,200.

Telephone recording pickup ($15–40)

It looks like a cellphone earpiece and it records phone calls by attaching to your phone and a tape or digital recorder. I found one at skymall.com. The site also carries a tape recording phone receiver priced at around $40 (used), $70 (new). Radio Shack's phone recorder costs only around $15 and achieves the same result. Cellphone recording devices are now available, too.

SafeGuardian GPS cellphone (around $100; monthly service, around $35)

Another gadget makes calling for help easy. A single red button calls for 24-hour help while the cellphone's internal GPS system pinpoints your exact location. Find this device here: www.safeguardian.com

Stash can diversion (around $15)

If you fear an intruder will grab your valuables, you might want to buy a "stash diversion" canister. They look like everything from cereal boxes to oatmeal containers but are hollow inside. Or create your own from empty food containers.

Video sunglasses (close to $4000)

I'm not sure anyone needs to own a pair of $4,000 sunglasses that don't have a Chanel label. But they are cool! This disguised device records up-close and personal encounters.

Pen recorder ($50–$100)

There are many common office supplies that mask audio bugs. A pen version has a recording device that lets you download the audio file to your desktop computer. The software should be included in the price. Most give you an hour of continuous recording time and are operated with a AAA battery.

Portable door alarm (around $20)

This small rectangular device makes a loud impression. You can carry it around with you or it can be converted to work on doors and windows, too.

Man's best friend

I didn't want to adopt a dog just for the sake of protection—but then a dog adopted me. A dog is one of the most reliable (and sweetest) alarm systems around.

Chapter Six

High-tech stalking gear and how to stop it

My computer gurgled and grinded with indigestion for months. It wasn't old, but it wasn't sprightly, either. As with all computers, it was outdated within six months, so I didn't give the noise a second thought. Then the strange behavior started. When I would open a file and begin typing, the program would freeze, then close. Many attempts to reopen were foiled by an invisible predator. I resorted to turning off my computer and restarting it. This occasionally fixed the problem. Most of the time, I would give up and call it a night. The culprit: cyberstalking.

I downloaded free virus and spyware applications on my computer, but anti-spyware is better at preventing problems than getting rid of them. In the end, my computer collapsed under the weight of the spyware using its memory.

Although I could never prove the man who stalked me was causing the computer problems, I knew. I knew because it was during this time that I was exploring online dating and both of my online accounts were hacked. A man with whom I had been corresponding was suddenly very offended. I also found my online profile maliciously altered. I knew. My computer knew.

But I didn't know soon enough. All victims of stalking should be aware of the high-tech savvy of many stalkers and the tools they use to invade your privacy. Your e-mail isn't private. Your instant messages aren't private. Your computer—if not protected—is a welcome mat for high-tech stalkers.

Computer software

Technology allows anyone to spy on your computer habits, record your every keystroke, record all your passwords, and take snapshots of your desktop. Some spyware programs can be remotely installed and monitored. They send automated e-mail logs of your keystrokes and Internet use. These programs can make your computer turn on and off, freeze or restart. Some spyware can turn on your computer's audio or video to record you while you sit at your computer.

In the case of solicited or unsolicited e-mail, *never* trust a gift horse or a RAT.

Trojan horses are programs usually attached to an incoming e-mail. When you open the attachment, it seems harmless. It may look like a letter or a simple form to fill out. But it may have a hidden program downloading to your computer. The program could send your personal files across the Internet or log your online activities.

A RAT (remote application tool) is computer software often delivered by a Trojan horse. A RAT usually has a much more sinister intention because once downloaded, it is used to control your computer from the safety of another computer. A RAT allows someone to read your e-mail, turn off your computer, record your keystrokes and open your personal files. RATs could also take pictures of your computer screen at timed intervals and send them to a stalker as e-mail attachments.

Keylogger applications can also be delivered by a Trojan horse. They record your every keystroke, including your username and password logins for every online account you use.

How to stop remote computer hacking tools

✓ **Restrict computer access with a username and password.**
Even if you're the only one who uses your computer, put up as many roadblocks as possible to restrict access.

✓ **Install a firewall.**
You can get a free and reputable firewall at www.zonealarm.com. You'll have to closely follow the links that wend through a maze of upsells for their premium product, but Zone Alarm is a solid and reliable firewall. Zone Alarm will warn you when your computer is calling out to the Internet, give you advice on what to do about it, and give you the opportunity to stop it from happening.

✓ **Change your e-mail address.**
Spyware is easily transmitted through e-mail. If a stalker doesn't know your e-mail address, he can't send a program to invade your computer.

✓ **Change your browser's security settings.**
On an Internet Explorer browser, go to the "tools," menu then "Internet options." Click on the security tab. Raise your browser's security level with the scroll button.

✓ **Do not download attachments, from anyone.**
This includes people you trust. Many spam e-mails include a "From:" e-mail address of a trusted friend or company. It's Internet fraud called "phishing." Often, phishing software scans your address book before sending

you an e-mail disguised as a missive from a trusted source.

✓ **Use anti-virus/anti-spyware software.**
Norton Utilities is a well-known and respected anti-virus software. Another well-known anti-virus/anti-spyware software company is Pest Patrol. Want something less expensive? Spyware Blaster doesn't eliminate existing spyware but it stops more from downloading on your computer. And it's free.

Here's where you can check for details and downloads:
www.javacoolsoftware.com/spywareblaster.html
www.safer-networking.org
www.spybot.com
www.pestpatrol.com

If you want to get an idea of the kind of malicious spyware out there, take a look at these unsettling hacker tools:
www.spy-patrol.com
www.computer-monitoring.com
www.4hiddenspycameras.com

✓ **Disconnect your computer.**
Always disconnect your computer from the phone line when it is not in use. Otherwise, an auto-dialer could turn on your computer while you're away, then secretly send a stalker your personal files. An auto-dialer also can be used by stalkers who want to make it seem like you called their phone. Then they might try to paint *you* as the stalker.

✓ **Start from scratch.**
With computers as cheap as they are, sometimes it's best to buy a new one if yours has been invaded. While using

my ex-boyfriend's computer, I found a slew of pornography. I also found a folder with my name on it. Inside were images of my "porn doubles," nude women who looked like me. There were other folders with other women's names, some of which I knew. Each was filled with the women's look-a-likes. Not sure what to make of this odd behavior, I downloaded some of the files onto my computer. A day hadn't passed before he asked why I'd copied his photos. I wondered how he knew. Later I found out he had installed spyware on my computer to monitor my every move.

✓ **Change all usernames and passwords.**

Gaining access to your private accounts can be just as devastating as physical stalking. Your identity can be sold, which leads to credit fraud that can haunt you for years and make it hard to buy a home or extend your credit. Access your private accounts from a safe computer and randomize your passwords with numbers and uppercase and lowercase letters.

GPS (logger version, around $900) (realtime version, around $1,500)

A Global Positioning Satellite (GPS) tracker is sometimes used to track teenagers, errant spouses or company cars. It is compact and can easily hide under the hood of a car.

Some GPS devices record travel patterns and the travel time between stops. So if you visit a friend, a stalker could tell how long you stayed. GPS loggers are not realtime devices; a logger must be detached from a vehicle and its information downloaded into a computer with the appropriate software to view the travel patterns.

With realtime GPS trackers, the operator (stalker) sits at his computer as the GPS tracker pinpoints a car's location. GPS devices are not affected by distance; they run via satellite.

Are you being tracked?

✓ Look for a black rectangular box under the hood, in the grill or underneath your car. Ask a technician to check for any foreign devices when you get an oil change.

Nanny Cam (around $70+)

Wireless cameras inside of your house could be intercepted by a high-tech stalker. Devices you thought were guarding you indoors can be used against you. A stalker can intercept the wireless signals from a security camera in your house with a receiver placed a quarter mile away. It's not illegal either. In many states, video surveillance is unaffected by wiretap laws.

Pull the plug

✓ Disable your indoor security cameras and receivers when they aren't needed.

Automatic phone recorder (around $100–$250)

This isn't an answering machine. It records all conversations on your land line. The device is triggered every time you pick up the receiver. Even if a stalker doesn't get access to your home, he can access your phone line via the outdoor jack the phone company uses when making service calls. This convenient outdoor phone jack attaches to your phone line, letting anybody make phone calls from your home or listen and record your conversations with an automatic phone recorder. This is why it's prudent to have a cellphone backup connected to an alarm system: Someone could block your land line from this outside jack. If it's blocked when the alarm sounds, the system will be blocked from calling the alarm station and police.

Protect your land line

✓ Place your outdoor jack under lock and key and check it frequently. Use a cellphone as your home number instead of a land line. If you have a security system, purchase a cellphone backup to compliment your land line system for around $200.

Concrete microphones (about $300)

Place this small device on a home's exterior wall and you can hear conversations going on inside. These devices work better with solid surfaces than plasterboard and studded walls. They work great in brick homes, but the device has to make contact with the wall to work.

How to stop concrete microphones

✓ Use floodlights on all corners of your home. Have phone conversations in a central room that does not share walls to the outdoors. Another alternative is white noise, a sound frequency that sounds like a soft hiss. It often is used to drown out noises such as planes and cars, but also can drown out your voice. You can buy white noise CDs from online sites for the same cost as a regular CD. Or opt for a white noise machine for $50–$100.

Cellphones equipped with cameras (about $100)

Sound familiar? Cellphones are on the list of items you should use for self-protection, but they also can be used against you. A cellphone's discrete size and tiny lens is easily hidden to record images of the unsuspecting. Many Web sites post cellphone images shot underneath girls' skirts and e-mailed by men who stalk them on subways or stairwells. Cellphones offer an easy transfer of these images through a wireless e-mail connection. Laws are only now being passed to make this a criminal offense. However, tracking the owner of these sites or the stalkers is difficult.

Most cellphone cameras take low-resolution photographs, but the newest cellphone cameras offer higher-resolution images. And some record short videos.

How to evade cellphone cameras

✓ Besides wearing pants, the best way to dodge cellphone pictures is to dodge a stalker. If you are inconsistent in your behavior, a stalker will have less chance of getting close to you.

Cellphones equipped with Bluetooth technology (about $100)

Bluetooth technology was developed for computerized devices to wirelessly transmit information. Personal digital assistants—or PDAs—use this technology to wirelessly transmit contact information into someone else's PDA with the touch of a button. The intent of this technology is convenience. It saves time to wirelessly transmit your contact information than to write it down. The problem is that it's just one more way a stalker can threaten a victim because messages can be wirelessly transmitted to your PDA without your consent.

BlueTooth technology requires someone to transmit a message 30 feet away. So although it is unlikely a stalker known intimately by a victim would get this close, such messages are untraceable and a danger to those stalked by strangers in crowded areas.

How to block Bluetooth technology

✓ Bluetooth technology is easily turned off in your cellphone's settings. Most people don't turn it off because they don't know what it is or that they even have it.

Fiber optic snake cameras (about $200)

It took me a year to figure out what my cat already knew on the nights I watched him bedazzled by what lurked in the dark at night outside my window: My ex-boyfriend watched me from my brightly lit windows in relative safety with a camera as his eyes. Peeping Toms no longer have to stick their face in a window and blow their cover at night. Today there are tiny fiber optic cameras with extendable arms that can do the peeping for them as they crouch a few feet below a window or door, out of sight, but with a clear picture of you.

How to stop it

✓ Put up opaque curtains or blinds. It's that simple!

Tactical Door Viewer ($150)

Peepholes allow a resident to look outside to see who's there. But a tactical door viewer turns the table. It looks like a small monocular that, when placed next to the exterior lens of a peephole refracts light, allowing a stalker to look indoors.

How to stop it

✓ Put masking tape on your peepholes when not in use.

Bogus computer peripherals ($150–$250)

Computer programs called keyloggers don't always come in the form of e-mail Trojans—seemingly innocuous e-mail attachments. Sometimes they disguise themselves as computer peripherals, like a cord connecting to your computer. For someone who doesn't know a lot about computers, a cord looks like a cord, and nothing else. And these "key ghosts" look like your ordinary keyboard cable. Inside they store a computer chip that records your every keystroke—and your anti-spyware can't detect it.

How to stop it

✓ Look for a cord with a small rectangular mid-section in the middle of its cord. It should be a conduit, connecting your computer to your keyboard cable.

Remailers

(most are free but there are remailer services such as www.hushmail.com)

Ever used an online dating service? Dating sites use remailers to mask the true e-mail address of the sender. This protects privacy. Most online remailers use online sites that send off an anonymous e-mail for them, like hushmail.com. These are known as "pseudo-remailers." True remailers are rare and typically used only by computer programmers.

Stalkers may use remailers to contact you. Using remailers lets a stalker harass you without revealing his e-mail address so you can't use e-mails as evidence in court.

How to stop anonymous e-mails from a stalker

✓ Proponents of online remailers say Internet service providers (ISPs) are like spies, logging every communication. But network tracking can work to your advantage. Remailers aren't tracked by ISPs, but the owner of a remailer site could be subpoenaed in a criminal case to reveal the true sender of the e-mail. To prevent such e-mail from reaching you, change your e-mail address. Only give your closest friends your private e-mail address. When filling out information about yourself for a new e-mail account, do not list any personally identifying information. In other words, lie!

Lock pick sets (about $50)

Picking locks is an art but can be learned by using any of the many manuals and tool kits sold.

How to stop a stalker from picking your lock

✓ Install police locks for a little extra protection. Popular in New York, these locks use steel bars that brace against the floor and door. Or, less secure but free, you can brace chairs against the knobs of entry doors. You could also buy a biometric lock, which allows access based on fingerprints. Or you might try locks that use card access. Both can be found at smarthome.com.

Telephone land lines ($0)

While being cross-examined for a bond hearing, a defense attorney, in ultra-Perry Mason style, brought out a phone bill documenting a phone call from my home to my ex-boyfriend's cellphone. The call was placed right after I filed charges for aggravated stalking, related to two incidents, one involving a friend being tailed by my ex-boyfriend. Both incidents were in violation of the protective order.

The phone call did not surprise me. Not because I made the call—I didn't—but because I knew he knew how to access my phone line. Although I never used my land line except as a DSL computer connection, the documented call, in a jury trial, was damaging to my case. The phone call made it seem as though I was calling him while claiming to be stalked.

Phone companies install outside jacks for their convenience—and, inadvertently, the convenience of stalkers. A cable connection for computer use is a better choice because you can use your cellphone to make phone calls. Today, alarm security systems can use a cellphone instead of a land line. If you have a security alarm system that uses a phone line, be aware that phone lines can be used to listen in on your calls as well as make phone calls you didn't actually make. Stalkers will use any tactic to discredit you. But remember: a cable connection can be cut, too; however, listening in on cellphone conversation, rather than a land line, is a lot more difficult.

How to stop a stalker from tampering with your phone line

✓ Either don't use land lines or lock up the phone company's outside jack. You might consider placing a motion detector or video camera where the outside phone jack is located.

Information Brokers ($50+)

Even if you change addresses to escape a stalker, he will likely find you. Information is abundant and for sale to anyone willing to pay for it. The information on your credit report—your name, current address and Social Security number, along with your credit card numbers—is not considered private and is sold to third-party companies. Companies resell private information to businesses and individuals willing to purchase it. Nobody cares how it is used.

How to stop your privacy from being invaded

- ✓ When you fill out a form, often it is put into a database. Don't leave a paper trail. Or in this case a digital trail. Your identity is recorded when calling toll-free phone numbers, too. Your phone number is mapped to your home address, along with your demographics. Your entire identity is unveiled with just one call. And your behavior is mapped together in a central repository.
- ✓ When you sign up for anything, lie about your contact information. Change your name. Buy a home as an LLC, a limited liability corporation, so your home sales deed cannot be traced directly to you. But if you do form a LLC when purchasing a house, make sure you put down another name and address as the contact information for the company because many states have public online databases searchable by name. If you don't *need* to give accurate information, don't!

Chapter Seven

Before You Go to Court

The low-tech in courtrooms

Pyrrhus, the ancient king of Epirius, was asked to fight against Roman invaders in southern Italy. He brought 25,000 men and 20 elephants to defend the small city against the Goliath. His victories were so costly, with the loss of so many men, that he remarked: "Another such victory and I shall be ruined." This is where the phrase "pyrrhic victory" originated. It is a victory with so much bloodshed and sorrow that there are no true victors. This is what it's like going through the American court system.

Sitting in a courtroom during domestic violence cases, you'll hear women's stories that are each chilling in their own way. There are male victims too, but this is rare. Affluent women are stalked, but you're more likely to see lower-income women just trying to get by. Most are trying to get out of a bad situation. Hearing their sad litany of problems, you wonder if they ever will.

In the course of three years, I'd been in a courtroom at least a dozen times. In between, I'd been shuffled from department to department, doing everything right, and losing my confidence that justice would prevail. But justice did prevail—and I would take all those steps again. As the gravity of the incidents increased, so did the advocacy on my behalf, and I didn't have to struggle as much to get someone's attention. The red tape turned into red carpet. But that didn't make it any easier. As crazy and backward as the system is, it is the best we have.

A little preparation can help you find justice. And with perseverance, you can prevail. So how can you get there sooner rather than later?

Rehearse your testimony

Rehearse what you might say on the witness stand the day before. Rehearsing is a good way to mentally prepare yourself. Imagine what a lawyer might ask you and how you would respond. Go over the important events in the case. Practice giving concise answers and making key points you feel are important. If you prepare, you are less likely to become emotional and more likely to sound credible.

Bring notes and documents to court

Bringing a list of bullet points you want to cover helps calm the nerves. I always brought notes, police reports and a copy of my protective order. I never looked at them, but I was glad the documents were there. Once a lawyer questioned whether I even held a permanent protective order. She asked for a copy during cross-examination. I had one on hand and offered it to her. She declined. Her tactic didn't work because I was prepared.

Keep your responses short

The sordid details of your story do not interest the judge or jury. However, they do interest the defense attorney. Defense attorneys are allowed to ask "leading questions" that suggest an answer during cross-examination. Since it is unlikely that a stalker will take the stand, opting instead to use his Fifth Amendment rights, you are likely to be the only one subjected to this kind of interrogation. "Isn't it true that you left your home at three o'clock?" is a leading question. The lawyers who represent you cannot ask leading questions. So the same question above would be rephrased: "At what time did you leave your home?"

Elaborate when given the chance. A defense attorney's questions are designed to keep your comments to a minimum. But be careful. Stick to the pertinent facts and events. On the stand, I nervously recounted the events. From watching the host of witnesses before me, I knew to keep it brief and to the point. Judges do not have time for drama. Leave out the myriad events that do not address the crime to avoid sounding scattered and diluting the key facts. Defense attorneys are interested in the off-topic details because it distracts the judge and jury from the relevant facts of a case.

Keep your emotions in check

Being nervous is natural. Do not let your anger or resentment sully your testimony. It makes you seem less credible. Control your emotions and concentrate on the facts. If you weep on the stand, you can't tell your story, and you may not get another chance. It is better to err on the side of being too dry and unemotional. Although I usually came off less sympathetically, remaining unemotional never worked against me, even in a jury trial where having a sympathetic personality often helps.

Do not react to the defense attorney's combative tactics

When I described myself as "paranoid" to express the mental toll of stalking, the defense attorney used it to her advantage. She accused me of suffering "paranoid" delusions. I responded calmly, didn't react, and explained that "paranoid" is an appropriate term to use after suffering years of stalking. I didn't succumb to an attorney's ploy to make me look unstable, and the judge didn't buy it, either.

On another occasion, a female attorney tried to discredit me as a scorned, vengeful woman. She was only doing her job, but she made me wonder whether there's a bit of the actor in every lawyer. "Hell hath no fury like a woman scorned," is how she began her closing argument. She concluded with another hackneyed phrase: "This woman should be on trial," her finger pointing at me. "This woman has come for her pound of flesh!" she concluded her impassioned closing remarks. You get the point. You'll feel like you're on trial. But that's how the system works. Everyone is innocent until proven guilty. And my ex-boyfriend was found guilty, in the end, despite the histrionics.

Opposing counsel's job is to upset you. Stand your ground but do not raise your voice. If you keep in mind that a defense attorney is only performing a job, you can answer the questions with composure. An attorney's job is to discredit you. They will try to make you seem emotionally unstable or deceptive. Don't let them.

Make it clear that you are afraid of what the stalker will do next

This is important. If a judge doesn't perceive the defendant as a threat, why should the court take action? There is no need to exaggerate. Just express your concern over what a stalker might do next.

Wear neutral-colored, conservative clothing

This is a courtroom, not a dance club. Wear business attire in dark shades. Wearing anything bright red makes you stand out. If color theory is true, you'll want to stay to shades of blue and gray. These colors communicate honesty and integrity.

Wear little, if any, makeup

Being attractive in court can work against you as well as for you. It is best to be unassuming. Jurors can interpret attractiveness as warranting stalking behavior or could find it to be unsympathetic. Be a bland, blank canvas. Communicate with your testimony, not your sense of style.

Address the judge as "Your Honor" and be respectful

During the jury trial for the criminal trespass charge against my ex-boyfriend, a polite judge suddenly became enraged, raising her voice in self-righteous defiance where there was a hum of voices in the back of the courtroom discussing the case. This prompted a diatribe on the decline of respect for authority. I'm not sure why judges fly off the handle, but I could hazard a guess: They've seen so much chaos that procedure and respect are essential to maintaining order. So be mindful. Show the judge respect even if events do not turn in your favor. You cannot win an argument with a judge, so don't even try.

Don't let the opposing attorney rush your testimony.

Remember that the defense attorney is trying to throw you off track. Remain calm and proceed at your own pace. There were many times when the opposing attorney asked a question and if I didn't answer exactly as I had on a former deposition, in even the slightest way, she would shove the deposition in my face to "refresh my memory." It was disconcerting to have her try to discredit me in this way. Her questions were not about facts. She merely wanted to make me look like a liar, so she brought up insignificant points in an attempt to sway the jury.

Look at the jury

As hard as I tried, it was difficult to look at strangers and share my personal hell in public. It is especially frustrating when there are so many rules. In some circumstances, relevant parts of the story are prohibited, and your testimony is limited by law. In the criminal trespass trial I couldn't mention the years of stalking, the other charges or anything in his past. My story was limited to a single event.

One male juror refused to look me in the eye. He was uncomfortable, and no doubt it was because the facts of the case were restricted. If the juror had known about the years and incidents strung along this tortuous path, the cold picture cast by the defense attorney would have crumbled in minutes. Nevertheless, the verdict was in my favor. But the hour and a half of deliberation made me nervous at the prospect of a "not guilty" verdict.

My lawyer turned to me before the trial and said, "Look at the jury. Don't be ashamed. Juries interpret lack of eye contact as deception." I looked at the jury, but not very often. The prosecutor was right. I was embarrassed for being in this situation, and having to relive my mistakes over and over and over. He told me not to be ashamed or embarrassed. But I was. I still am.

The high-tech in courtrooms

The courtroom is a fickle arena in which evidence that seems overwhelming is dismissed as circumstantial. Any evidence is welcome, but some evidence is a lot more convincing.

Audiotapes

Federal law requires that there is at least the informed consent of one party when a conversation is taped. Some state laws require the informed consent of all parties. Find out what your state law is. Single-consent states only require that *you* knew the conversation was taped for it to be admissible in court.

For more information on audiotaping laws in your state visit this Web site: www.rcfp.org/taping

Videotapes

Videotape laws are much more lenient, and therefore videotapes will likely be allowed as evidence. A time stamp makes the evidence much more convincing.

Photographs

Carry a disposable camera with you. Cameras with time stamps are more convincing evidence in court.

E-mails or handwritten notes

I brought in a handwritten note I found taped to my garbage can. This helped convince a judge to grant me a permanent restraining order. After a year of continued harassment, the note was another sign of stalking, because my ex-boyfriend did not use the U.S. Postal Service. He came to my house. E-mails are also good evidence today, if you can verify the e-mail address was used by the accused.

Computer stalking

If you testify that your computer was "hijacked" by hacker software, you'll need expert testimony to back this claim. Although my computer was monitored, I could never prove it. The cost of experts can run high. This is why an ounce of prevention is a better option. You may want to check whether your state has a special crime unit dedicated to cyber crimes. Such crimes are becoming more prevalent as demand for more sophisticated law enforcement increases with the growth of technology.

Chapter Eight

Whom to avoid

During hard times, there will always be thoughtless people who can drag you down even more. But don't let them.

Fair-weather friends

They'll want every detail of your personal drama, but if the events ever touch their lives they'd sooner cut off a limb than help. I had such a friend during my trials, both literal and figurative. While a restraining order was in place, he sat down to talk to the man who stalked me. He was kind enough to tell me about the meeting afterwards. But when he realized it was a clear violation of the TPO—because he acted as a third party in relaying information to me—he was swift to beg out with the standard, "I don't want to get involved."

Government workers

I mistook the victim's assistance division of the county government as a resource. The only assistance it gave me was a clearer realization of how dysfunctional and useless government workers can be. Yes, the one division that was supposed to assist me was the most useless.

When dealing with government workers, it is helpful to realize they tend to work against, rather than for, you. Every time I step inside a government building, I know I'm going to get shuffled from department to department by workers whose job seemingly is not to serve you but to get rid of you. For those of you with positive experiences with the system, please write in. No doubt your experience will be regarded akin to a sighting of Elvis. For the rest of you, be vigilant, keep asking questions and move on if you doubt the answers you get.

After being turned down several times by the victim's assistance office, I visited a Legal Aid office and got an impromptu meeting. I didn't qualify for legal services because my salary was too high, but I did get to speak with an advocate who, after a few phone calls, set up a meeting for me with people from the office that had refused to deal with me before. A year later, I walked in to Legal Aid again and spoke with the same woman. She helped me find legal representation. Even though I didn't qualify for their services, they shared their knowledge and were advocates.

Clueless sympathizers

During my ordeal, a relative of mine sympathized with the stalker. My ex-boyfriend convinced my relative, in private conversations, that I should keep him on my cellphone plan for another week. This led to one of the stupidest decisions I ever made. Granting him an extension led to more trouble in court. If I had listened to my gut, and not the misguided sympathies of a relative, I could have spared myself the grief.

Misinformed miscreants

While in the waiting room of the victim's assistance office I met a male "friend" of a woman who was seeking help. He said his friend's boyfriend had gone crazy. His conclusion? She must have "done something" to provoke his anger. This is by far the most common conclusion of the uninformed. I looked at him dumbfounded, holding back my disgust.

Another chance encounter with insensitivity took place in my home. While getting my security system upgraded I explained to the electrical technician the problem—that the man breaking in was an electrician who could dismantle and circumvent a security system. His response was the same: "What did you do to him?" Not only was his opinion unprofessional but he topped his visit off by asking me out for a date. So not only was I worried that my ex-boyfriend would dismantle my alarm system, now I was worried that the security technician knew how to turn it off.

Know-it-alls

During your ordeal, you'll probably run into some "know-it-alls," too. These friends and family members will tell you what to do and how to handle situations. They'll blame you for the events in the process. These are bullying, disempowering people. Avoid their speeches about how you should act or what you should do. There is nothing empowering about other people telling you what to do. And even though someone—a friend, a counselor, an advocate, a parent—might act like they have all the answers, it's your life—and your decisions.

Of course, some family and friends give good advice. Some people will surprise you, pleasantly. Others will disappoint you, unexpectedly. One friend will be hysterical. Another will come to your aid without question. Others will chide you: "I hope you learned your lesson." But some will stand by your side.

We all make good and bad choices. Maybe you didn't see the red flags, ignored growing suspicions or never knew what a healthy relationship was supposed to be like. But you are not responsible for the behavior of another. It isn't you who is making him stalk. It is the stalker's obsession and need for control that makes him a stalker.

The self-absorbed

My ex-boyfriend infiltrated my neighbors. While the neighborhood was fighting a zoning battle, they used my ex-boyfriend for his expertise on zoning although he never lived in the neighborhood and they knew I had a restraining order against him. I was told by the community leader and a neighbor to "put our differences aside" for the good of the community.

Attorneys

When I first got a temporary protective order, I was dragged back into court. The attorney argued that my ex-boyfriend wasn't properly served the TPO. In a knee-jerk panic at the prospect of being cross-examined by his attorney, I hired my own for a flat fee of $1,200. This was a colossal waste of money.

Most of the time, you don't need a lawyer to get a protective order. Domestic violence centers will help you fill out the paperwork and get you a lawyer for free if you don't have one.

Protective orders are rarely refused. Judges don't want to be held responsible if they guess wrong. Besides, the order is not a mark on the defendant's record. It becomes a criminal case only if the person violates terms of the protective order. The accused just has to stay away. Seems simple enough, but it is amazing how hard it is for a stalker to restrain his need to regain control. More than 60 percent of protective orders are violated.

Attorneys sometimes are needed. During the civil lawsuit my ex-boyfriend brought against me, the bills piled up. When you pay an attorney, you'll wonder what merits so much money an hour when you seem to be doing all the work. You'll make copies, run around, log the events and even remind him what your name is. You'd think for $200 an hour an attorney could remember the pertinent facts of your case. Feel lucky if you land an attorney who is at least cordial.

It's a challenge finding a good attorney if you wind up facing a civil lawsuit. The attorney you want may be too busy or not interested. Someone else may request $100–$200 for a "consultation" to review your case. New online services, such as www.legalmatch.com, may save you time in your search. You supply a quick synopsis of your case and the hourly rate you prefer to pay. When an attorney fits your criteria and is interested in your case you receive an e-mail and can initiate contact.

If you don't get sued by your stalker, and most of you won't, you may never have to pay for an attorney. Attorneys represent the state—and therefore, you—in prosecuting crimes such as stalking, peeping Tom and criminal trespass. The state regards these offenses as crimes against the state. You are a witness for the state. A victim's advocate also is appointed free of charge.

The stalker's friends and family

Do not call or write to a stalker's friends or family, no matter how tempting it may be to argue your point. It's a waste of energy. They become dangerous sources of information for stalkers and you're feeding them more information. Anything you say can be used against you in court. Don't be so blind as to think you can change their minds. You can't.

Chapter Nine

How to Avoid a Stalker

WHO STALKS?

Studies show that most stalkers are of above average intelligence, convincing and crafty. Nearly 90 percent of stalkers are men, and the majority of their victims are women. Over half of stalking victims know their stalkers, and the stalking is commonly the result of an intimate breakup. Stalking lasts for about two years on average. Seventy-six percent of women killed were stalked by their killer; this percentage goes up for women who were physically abused by their stalker.

Simple obsessional stalkers

Simple obsessional stalkers are the most common type of stalkers and are likely known by the victims, due to an intimate relationship. The obsession often occurs after a breakup or other perceived wrong. Revenge leads to attempts to intimidate or gain control of the victim's life. Or sometimes the action is seen as attempts at reconciliation. The simple obsessional stalker is typically a middle-aged man who has a personality disorder. This type of person poses the greatest physical threat. He blames the victim for the perceived wrongs. Many have a history of being unable to form lasting relationships. Criminal or drug-related activity may be part of the picture, too.

Love obsessional stalkers

Love obsessional stalkers likely suffer from mental disorders such as bipolar personality or schizophrenia and form a fixation on someone they believe to be their perfect match. Generally, they have not been intimate with their victims, who may not even know them.

Erotomanic stalkers

Erotomanic stalkers think their victims are in love with them. In most cases, these stalkers fixate on someone in a higher social status. They are more likely to be women who form fantasies about their victim's affections.

~ ~ ~

How can you avoid stalkers?

My story begins the way a lot of women's stories do. I met someone and failed to recognize the red flags until the house of cards came tumbling down. The best advice I can give anyone, is an ounce of prevention: Pay attention to red flags.

AVOIDING STALKERS THE LOW-TECH WAY

If you're uncomfortable, there's a reason for it

If you read the pamphlets in your state's victim assistance office, you'll likely find them simplistic at best. They pander to the lowest common denominator and offer advice that's little more than common sense. But they usually include one very helpful piece of advice: Know your limits.

The most important thing to remember is to never accept a situation in which you feel uncomfortable—whether it is where a date is taking you or whether you should live together. Always, always trust your gut feeling and never play along to get along. Your intuition is probably the most important radar you possess. If you feel uncomfortable, it doesn't matter what anyone else thinks. This is your life. Do not talk yourself into a situation that doesn't feel right for you. You're the one who matters.

Stalkers aren't just solitary weirdos

I read a lot of pamphlets describing stalkers as socially inept, but when I spoke to lawyers and victim's advocates, they agreed that most stalkers are charismatic and smart. Stalkers often have many friends. They are often regarded as gregarious and charming. Maybe because they know people so well, they can easily manipulate them. They are people persons.

People sympathize with their sad tales. Once arrested, friends and neighbors often say a stalker was "such a nice guy" or "he wouldn't hurt a fly." There is a reason for this. The criminal, in this case a stalker, is a well-liked, outgoing fellow who uses his personality to gain alliances and get an army of supporters.

My ex-boyfriend's charisma helped gloss over glaring problems. His description of a tumultuous past relationship became a convincing hook, and not the red flag it should have been. He confessed early to his troubling past with a boyish earnestness I took for truth. His group of female friends was extensive, so I accepted his story. How can a man have so many female friends if he is a danger to them? The answer: He duped them, too.

Obsessive behavior—also known as "perfectionism"—can signify controlling behavior

There were other signs that I dismissed as eccentricities. He was fastidious to a flaw. He took detailed notes. These were not just random notations, but notes on all receipts, carefully tucked into dated envelopes. He even kept a diary that lacked inner thoughts but commented on the day in a series of bullet points of mundane daily rituals. His attention to detail was a benefit and a curse. He could account for almost everything in minute detail but wasn't able to roll with the punches. He was controlling.

Not only did he control his day in a long paper trail, but meals had to be elaborate, not sparse, and our days were outlined with a weekly "to do" list that weighted the importance of each task in order of greatest need. I'm sure you are thinking, "My God, how annoying!" It was very annoying. I tolerated it because he convinced me his intentions were in my best interest.

His controlling nature manifested itself slowly. Where are you going? How long will you be? Who will you be with? These questions are normal conversation for most couples who honestly want to know where their loved one is. But knowing where someone is and keeping tabs on them are two different things. When I worked late, he became irritated. When I went to a movie, he wanted to go along and moped if he was left out, making me feel guilty for wanting to visit a friend alone. Even if you're performing simple, mundane tasks, a controlling person might want to do those things with you. It feels like prison, and you are tied to your cellmate.

Couples should be able to do their own tasks separately without fear or recrimination. If it makes you feel uncomfortable then something is wrong. Stalkers need control. They live in a world of fear: fear of loss, of losing control, of losing you. They'll manipulate through arguments, threats and recriminations.

Too much dependence

The more time passed, the more I found myself entwined financially and logistically to a man I wasn't committed to marrying. Don't act married if you aren't. What your mother says is true: Never live with a man before marriage. I'm not saying this because I'm old-fashioned, I'm saying this because in today's legal climate, another person's problems and finances become your problems and put you at risk.

In a few years, our finances became increasingly tied together. Financial dependency may be a natural product of marriage, but when you are just dating or living with someone, combined finances can mean trouble ahead. When someone wants to freely co-mingle your money with his, think twice.

The need to always win is not a winning combination

My ex-boyfriend never hit me, but there are plenty of other aggressive ways to dominate. The more troubled our relationship became, the more we fought. And the more we fought, the more intense and tiresome these arguments became. I never left a fight without feeling emotionally exhausted and bruised. Our fights were a never-ending play that cycled over and over again. Yet, he always won the argument. Not because he was right, but because he had an inexhaustible stamina to drill and battle until I acquiesced. I bowed to his will, inevitably feeling dissatisfied and guilty. I was never understanding enough and never seemingly right. Our fights escalated, and his willfulness became even more unrelenting.

Near the end of our relationship, I remember hiring an outside contractor to refinish my hardwood floors. The contractor was being paid from my bank account. My ex-boyfriend didn't like the contractor's work, and said it should be redone. I didn't agree. I didn't want to pay more to get it done. A night of fighting ensued. In tears, I relented. When I refused to participate in the work, he'd remind me that "we decided to refinish the hardwood floors together." In his mind, I had agreed. All that mattered to him was that he got his way. My decision was his decision and "we" were of one will—his.

If someone makes you feel inadequate because you are never understanding enough or never thoughtful enough, it is likely that he is the thoughtless one. The person who always wins the argument is someone who always wants to win. Someone who always wants to win just might stop at nothing if you leave. Their type of unrelenting action in arguments can become unrelenting action to win you back. But remember: Their action isn't about you, about wanting you back or about love. It is about control.

Artful dodging should remain in playschool dodge ball

Throughout the relationship, problems were often met with excuses. His bad credit wasn't important. His late-night computer use was "work," not a pornography obsession, as I later discovered. His disinterest in finding a job was countered with guilt trips. I wasn't supportive enough, he told me. I wasn't patient enough.

I didn't realize that dodging responsibility is common among stalkers. I always thought it would get better. That's what he kept telling me. That's what I wanted to believe. Guess what? It never did.

AVOIDING STALKERS THE HIGH-TECH WAY

One way to avoid a stalker is to never date a known stalker. Although doing a background check doesn't guarantee you won't be stalked, at least you could get the peace of mind that comes with doing some research.

Criminal records are public record and are becoming more accessible online. Public records include everything from home sales to marriages, deaths, voter registration, criminal records, lawsuits, sex offender registries, tax liens, bankruptcies and births. Online background check companies take this free public information and sell it to you for $40–$100 or more. But be careful when choosing an online data broker. There are so many, it is hard to tell which are reputable. And not all information is online so something you might want to know could fall through the cracks.

If you suspect someone of half truths, uncovering public records could tip the balance. But before paying an online search you may want to search online yourself. First try a Web search using key words that include your county you live in with other keywords like "court," "superior," "public," and "records." Some counties have highly sophisticated Web sites you can surf for free.

But some government sites fall short. You may need to pay for an online service.

Free online sites include:

www.publicrecordfinder.com
www.ire.org/datalibrary/databases
Home sales deeds: (www.domania.com)
Phone numbers/reverse lookup: (www.switchboard.com)

Online knowledge broker sites:

Both of these companies charge a fee and specialize in merging government and business databases for a composite view of someone's credit history and criminal background.
www.knowx.com
www.whoishe.com

Abika, another pay service, extends its database reach to a person's online activity in chat rooms, bulletin boards and online activities. This is useful for finding out the secret proclivities of a prospective intimate (i.e., pornography habits).
www.abika.com

Chapter Ten

What Next?

Before the jury trial for the criminal trespass charge against my ex-boyfriend, I asked the prosecutor, "Why do I have to be there? All it serves to do is beat me up. He's in jail. He's been in jail for seven months. He'll only get time served." The attorney slowly replied, "It gives you your day in court." I squelched a laugh. "I've been given that opportunity about 15 times! When will it end?"

When will it end? No one knows except the stalker. Although the trial for criminal trespass went in my favor, my ex-boyfriend appealed immediately after sentencing. Appeals work for stalkers in two ways: If you later go to court to face other charges, the prosecutor cannot mention the conviction if it's being appealed. Appeals also give the stalker more access to you, your attention and your time.

The civil lawsuit my ex-boyfriend launched against me was dismissed with prejudice after two years of crippling legal fees. I thought my financial woes were over. Then I received notice of an appeal of the suit, which meant more legal fees and potential battles. In the end, he lost that battle, too.

Some experts parrot this advice to stalking victims: "Run. Don't walk." But what happens when there is nowhere left to run or hide? What if you don't want to change your job or life? How can moving help if the stalker knows where you work? All of this likely does little more than delay future abuse.

~ ~ ~

Some years back on a crowded subway car I sat listless and unflinching, lined up tightly beside other New Yorkers along for the ride. Out of this dead calm, a man raised his voice and threatened to beat up his girlfriend, who sat meekly beside him in tears. His threat was clear. He was going to teach her a lesson when they got home. Everyone on the train held their tongue, keeping a steady eye on the floor, hoping his threats would stop. The man threatened her again. She continued to cry. He raised his voice again, as if they were alone, and unable to hold back my disdain, I broke the promise among subway riders, the promise to mind my own business. "Leave her alone," I mumbled, holding back my anger.

"Why don't you mind your own business?" he said.

"You made it my business when you made threats in public," I said, staring back at him. Our eyes locked the remainder of the ride. No one was hurt, and I left the train at my stop with the small dignity of speaking up.

When I recounted the subway event, I was verbally assaulted by victim's rights advocates who felt my intervention endangered the woman. Their arguments fell on my ears like hollow reason. The woman's life was in danger before I sat on the train. The woman's life was in danger after I left the train. The woman's life was in danger if I had never even stepped aboard the train. How many times do we have to bite our tongues before we speak out? How many people must live in fear before we fight back?

I feel the same today.

"These people kill people" was the reply a victim's advocate gave me when I told her I wasn't going to sell my home and move to get away from my stalker. Fear is a stalker's weapon. Intimidation is a stalker's tool. I'll leave when I'm ready to leave and not a minute sooner, I told her, words I stand by even after three years of battle.

I don't know when it will end. But I do know I'll be standing when it does. And with the help of high-tech devices and low-tech know-how, you, too, can fight back, protect your privacy and regain control of your life.

Additional Resources

Want to learn more?

Did you find this book helpful? Visit **dianeglass.com** and swap ideas or share your personal stories with other stalking victims. On dianeglass.com you will also learn about the newest strategies and spyware technology.

www.dianeglass.com

stalkingbook@gmail.com

978-0-595-38332-0
0-595-38332-7

Printed in the United States
67124LVS00006B/3